Pocket Pal®

Knock Knock Jokes

hinkler

Pocket Pal®

Knock Knock Jokes

hinkler

Published by Hinkler Books Pty Ltd
45–55 Fairchild Street
Heatherton Victoria 3202 Australia
www.hinkler.com.au

© Hinkler Books Pty Ltd 2010

Cover Illustration: Rob Kiely
Illustrations: Glen Singleton
Prepress: Splitting Image
Typesetting: MPS Limited

ISBN: 978 1 7418 5788 7

Printed and bound in China

Knock Knock
Who's there?
Alison!
Alison who?
Alison to the radio!

Knock Knock
Who's there?
Ahmed!
Ahmed who?
Ahmed a mistake! I think I want the house next door!

Knock Knock
Who's there?
Avon!
Avon who?
Avon you to open the door!

Knock Knock
Who's there?
Abba!
Abba who?
Abba banana!

Knock Knock

Who's there?

Aida!

Aida who?

Aida whole box of cookies and now I feel sick!

Knock Knock

Who's there?

Artichokes!

Artichokes who?

Artichokes when he eats too fast!

Knock Knock
Who's there?
Army!
Army who?
Army and you still friends?

Knock Knock
Who's there?
Aitch!
Aitch who?
Do you need a tissue?

Knock Knock
Who's there?
Arch!
Arch who?
Bless you!

Knock Knock
Who's there?
Alota!
Alota who?
Alota good this is doing me!

Knock Knock

Who's there?

Alaska!

Alaska who?

Alaska one more time. Please let me in!

Knock Knock

Who's there?

Alaska!

Alaska who?

Alaska no questions! You tella no lies!

Knock Knock

Who's there?

Alf!

Alf who?

Alf all if you don't catch me!

Knock Knock

Who's there?

Alex!

Alex who?

Alex-plain later, just let me in!

Knock Knock
Who's there?
Abbot!
Abbot who?
Abbot you don't know who this is!

Knock Knock
Who's there?
Accordion!
Accordion who?
Accordion to the TV,
it's going to rain tomorrow!

Knock Knock
Who's there?
Amos!
Amos who?
Amosquito!

Knock Knock
Who's there?
Anna!
Anna who?
Annather mosquito!

Knock Knock
Who's there?
Adore!
Adore who?
Adore is between us, open up!

Knock Knock
Who's there?
Adore!
Adore who?
Adore is for knocking on!

Knock Knock

Who's there?

Ammonia!

Ammonia who?

Ammonia little girl who can't reach the doorbell!

Knock Knock

Who's there?

Abe!

Abe who?

Abe C D E F G H!

Knock Knock

Who's there?

Arncha!

Arncha who?

Arncha going to let me in? It's freezing out here!

Knock Knock

Who's there?

Albert!

Albert who?

Albert you don't know who this is?

Knock Knock

Who's there?

Avon!

Avon who?

Avon you to be my wife!

Knock Knock

Who's there?

Abbey!

Abbey who?

Abbey stung me
on the nose!

14

Knock Knock

Who's there?

Abbey!

Abbey who?

Abbey hive is where honey is made!

Knock Knock

Who's there?

Armageddon!

Armageddon who?

Armageddon out of here!

Knock Knock

Who's there?

Abbott!

Abbott who?

Abbott time you opened this door!

Knock Knock
Who's there?
Acute!
Acute who?
Acute little boy!

Knock Knock
Who's there?
Adder!
Adder who?
Adder you get in here?

Knock Knock
Who's there?
Arthur!
Arthur who?
Arthur anymore jelly beans in the jar?

18

Knock Knock

Who's there?

Ahab!

Ahab who?

Ahab to go to the toilet now!
Quick, open the door!

Knock Knock

Who's there?

Althea!

Althea who?

Althea later, alligator!

Knock Knock
Who's there?
Abyssinia!
Abyssinia who?
Abyssinia when I get back!

Knock Knock
Who's there?
Adair!
Adair who?
Adair once, but I'm bald now!

Knock Knock
Who's there?
Boo!
Boo who?
What are you crying about?

21

Knock Knock

Who's there?

Boo!

Boo who?

Here's a hanky, now let me in!

Knock Knock

Who's there?

Ben!

Ben who?

Ben knocking on the door
all afternoon!

Knock Knock

Who's there?

Ben!

Ben who?

Ben down and look through the letter slot!

Knock Knock

Who's there?

Bab!

Bab who?

Baboons are a type of ape!

Knock Knock
Who's there?
Bark!
Bark who?
Barking up the wrong tree!

Knock Knock
Who's there?
Butcher!
Butcher who?
Butcher little arms
around me!

Knock Knock

Who's there?

Barry!

Barry who?

Barry the treasure where no one will find it!

Knock Knock

Who's there?

Bashful!

Bashful who?

I'm too shy to tell you!

Knock Knock

Who's there?

Bat!

Bat who?

Batman and Robin are superheroes!

Knock Knock

Who's there?

Bowl!

Bowl who?

Bowl me over!

Knock Knock
Who's there?
Beck!
Beck who?
Beckfast is ready!

Knock Knock
Who's there?
Beet!
Beet who?
Beets me! I've forgotten my own name!

Knock Knock

Who's there?

Butcher!

Butcher who?

Butcher left leg in, butcher left leg out . . .

Knock Knock
Who's there?
Bear!
Bear who?
Bearer of glad tidings!

Knock Knock
Who's there?
Beryl!
Beryl who?
Roll out the Beryl!

Knock Knock
Who's there?
Bjorn!
Bjorn who?
Bjorn free!

Knock Knock
Who's there?
Bolton!
Bolton who?
Bolton the door! That's why
I can't get in!

Knock Knock

Who's there?

Bernadette!

Bernadette who?

Bernadette my lunch! Now I'm starving!

Knock Knock

Who's there?

Butcher!

Butcher who?

Butcher money where your mouth is!

Knock Knock
Who's there?
Betty!
Betty who?
Betty late than never!

Knock Knock
Who's there?
Betty!
Betty who?
Betty let me in or there'll be trouble!

Knock Knock
Who's there?
Bach!
Bach who?
Bach of chips!

Knock Knock
Who's there?
Back!
Back who?
Back off, I'm going to force my way in!

Knock Knock

Who's there?

Bacon!

Bacon who?

Bacon a cake for
your birthday!

Knock Knock

Who's there?

Bart!

Bart who?

Bartween you and me, I'm sick
of standing in the cold!

Knock Knock
Who's there?
Bee!
Bee who?
Bee careful!

Knock Knock
Who's there?
Beef!
Beef who?
Beefair now!

Knock Knock

Who's there?

Butter!

Butter who?

Butter wear a coat when you come out. It's cold!

Knock Knock

Who's there?

Brie!

Brie who?

Brie me my supper!

Knock Knock

Who's there?

Barbie!

Barbie who?

Barbie Q!

Knock Knock

Who's there?

Ben Hur!

Ben Hur who?

Ben Hur almost an hour so let me in!

Knock Knock

Who's there?

Beth!

Beth who?

Beth wisheth, thweetie!

Knock Knock

Who's there?

Beth!

Beth who?

Bethlehem is where Jesus was born!

Knock Knock

Who's there?

Burglar!

Burglar who?

Burglars don't knock!

Knock Knock
Who's there?
Baby Owl!
Baby Owl who?
Baby Owl
see you later,
maybe I won't!

Knock Knock
Who's there?
Bea!
Bea who?
Because I said so!

Knock Knock

Who's there?

Bart!

Bart who?

Bart-enders serve drinks!

Knock Knock

Who's there?

Ben!

Ben who?

Ben away a long time!

Knock Knock
Who's there?
Biafra!
Biafra who?
Biafra'id, be very afraid!

Knock Knock
Who's there?
Boxer!
Boxer who?
Boxer tricks!

Knock Knock
Who's there?
Bean!
Bean who?
Bean working too hard lately!

Knock Knock
Who's there?
Barbara!
Barbara who?
Barbara black sheep, have you any wool ...

BAA..! I have a very woolly jumper

Knock Knock
Who's there?
Bella!
Bella who?
Bella bottom trousers!

Knock Knock
Who's there?
Bean!
Bean who?
Bean to any movies lately?

Knock Knock

Who's there?

Cargo!

Cargo who?

Cargo beep beep!

Knock Knock

Who's there?

Caterpillar!

Caterpillar who?

Cat-er-pillar of feline society!

Knock Knock

Who's there?

C-2!

C-2 who?

C-2 it that you remember me next time!

Knock Knock

Who's there?

Cameron!

Cameron who?

Cameron film are what you need to take pictures!

Knock Knock
Who's there?
Cornflakes!
Cornflakes who?
I'll tell you tomorrow, it's a cereal!

Knock Knock
Who's there?
Celia!
Celia who?
Celia later
alligator!

Knock Knock

Who's there?

Carl!

Carl who?

Carload of furniture for you!
Where do you want it?

Knock Knock

Who's there?

Chuck!

Chuck who?

Chuck if I've left my keys inside!

Knock Knock
Who's there?
Carrie!
Carrie who?
Carrie on with what you're doing!

Knock Knock
Who's there?
Carson!
Carson who?
Carsonogenic!

Knock Knock

Who's there?

Closure!

Closure who?

Closure mouth when you're eating!

Knock Knock

Who's there?

Chicken!

Chicken who?

Chicken your pocket! My keys might be there!

Knock Knock

Who's there?

Claire!

Claire who?

Claire the snow from your path or someone will have an accident!

Knock Knock

Who's there?

Cologne!

Cologne who?

Cologne me names won't get you anywhere!

Knock Knock

Who's there?

Cosi!

Cosi who?

Cosi had to!

K_{nock} Knock
Who's there?
Crispin!
Crispin who?
Crispin juicy is how I like my chicken!

K_{nock} Knock
Who's there?
Caesar!
Caesar who?
Caesar quickly,
before she gets
away!

Knock Knock
Who's there?
Carrie!
Carrie who?
Carrie me inside, I'm exhausted!

Knock Knock
Who's there?
Carlotta!
Carlotta who?
Carlotta trouble when it breaks down!

Knock Knock
Who's there?
Cantaloupe!
Cantaloupe who?
Cantaloupe with you tonight!

Knock Knock
Who's there?
Carmen!
Carmen who?
Carmen get it!

Knock Knock
Who's there?
Cows go!
Cows go who?
Cows go 'moo', not 'who'!

Knock Knock

Who's there?

Cattle!

Cattle who?

Cattle always purr when you stroke it!

Knock Knock

Who's there?

Cecil!

Cecil who?

Cecil have music where ever she goes!

Knock Knock
Who's there?
Caesar!
Caesar who?
Caesar jolly
good fellow!

Knock Knock
Who's there?
Celeste!
Celeste who?
Celeste time I come around here!

Knock Knock
Who's there?
Colin!
Colin who?
Colin all cars! Colin all cars!

Knock Knock
Who's there?
Cheese!
Cheese who?
Cheese a jolly good fellow!

Knock Knock
Who's there?
Cook!
Cook who?
One o'clock!

Knock Knock
Who's there?
Curry!
Curry who?
Curry me back home please!

Knock Knock
Who's there?
Cash!
Cash who?
Are you a nut?

Knock Knock
Who's there?
Canoe!
Canoe who?
Canoe come
out and play
with me?

Knock Knock

Who's there?

Dingo!

Dingo who?

Dingo anywhere on the weekend!

Knock Knock

Who's there?

Dat!

Dat who?

Dat's all folks!

64

Knock Knock
Who's there?
Dwayne!
Dwayne who?
Dwayne the bathtub before I drown!

Knock Knock
Who's there?
Dale!
Dale who?
Dale come if you ask dem!

Knock Knock

Who's there?

Debate!

Debate who?

Debate goes on de hook if you want to catch de fish!

Knock Knock

Who's there?

Dad!

Dad who?

Dad 2 and 2 to get 4!

Knock Knock
Who's there?
Data!
Data who?
Data remember!

Knock Knock
Who's there?
Denise!
Denise who?
Denise are
between the waist
and the feet!

Knock Knock

Who's there?

Des!

Des who?

Des no bell! That's why I'm knocking!

Knock Knock

Who's there?

Diego!

Diego who?

Diegos before the B!

Knock Knock

Who's there?

Dish!

Dish who?

Dish is getting boring!
Open the door!

Knock Knock

Who's there?

Don!

Don who?

Don just stand there! Open the door!

Knock Knock

Who's there?

Diss!

Diss who?

Diss is a recorded message! 'Knock Knock, Knock Knock, Knock Knock.'

Knock Knock

Who's there?

Diss!

Diss who?

Diss is ridiculous! Let me in!

Knock Knock
Who's there?
Disguise!
Disguise who?
Disguise the limit!

Knock Knock
Who's there?
Diesel!
Diesel who?
Diesel help with
your cold!
Take two every four hours!

Knock Knock

Who's there?

Doctor!

Doctor who?

That's right!

I just feel SO DOWN!

Knock Knock

Who's there?

Despair!

Despair who?

Despair tyre
is flat!

Knock Knock

Who's there?

Don!

Don who?

Donkey rides! Donkey rides!
Only five dollars a ride!

Knock Knock

Who's there?

Duncan!

Duncan who?

Duncan disorderly!

Knock Knock
Who's there?
Dishes!
Dishes who?
Dishes a very bad joke!

Knock Knock
Who's there?
Dan!
Dan who?
Dan Druff!

Knock Knock
Who's there?
Danielle!
Danielle who?
Danielle so loud, I can hear you!

Knock Knock
Who's there?
Daryl!
Daryl who?
Daryl never be
another you!

Knock Knock
Who's there?
Dave!
Dave who?
Dave-andalised our house!

Knock Knock
Who's there?
Datsun!
Datsun who?
Datsun old joke!

Knock Knock

Who's there?

Euripides!

Euripides who?

Euripides pants, Eumenides pants!

Knock Knock

Who's there?

Empty!

Empty who?

Empty V (MTV)!

Knock Knock
Who's there?
Ella!
Ella who?
Ella-mentary, my dear fellow!

Knock Knock
Who's there?
Ellie!
Ellie who?
Ellie-phants
never forget!

Knock Knock
Who's there?
Ellis!
Ellis who?
Ellis between K and M!

Knock Knock
Who's there?
Elsie!
Elsie who?
Elsie you down at the mall!

Knock Knock

Who's there?

Europe!

Europe who?

Europen the door so I can come in!

Knock Knock

Who's there?

Effie!

Effie who?

Effie'd known you were coming he'd have stayed at home!

Knock Knock
Who's there?
Eliza!
Eliza who?
Eliza wake at night thinking about you!

Knock Knock
Who's there?
Evan!
Evan who?
Evan you should know who I am!

Knock Knock

Who's there?

Freeze!

Freeze who?

Freeze a jolly good fellow!

Knock Knock
Who's there?
Fantasy!
Fantasy who?
Fantasy a walk on the beach?

Knock Knock
Who's there?
Ferdie!
Ferdie who?
Ferdie last time open the door!

Knock Knock

Who's there?

Fanny!

Fanny who?

Fanny the way you keep asking,
'Who's there?'

Knock Knock

Who's there?

Figs!

Figs who?

Figs the doorbell, it's been broken
for ages!

Knock Knock
Who's there?
Foster!
Foster who?
Foster than a speeding bullet!

Knock Knock
Who's there?
Francis!
Francis who?
Francis the home of the Eiffel Tower!

Knock Knock
Who's there?
Frank!
Frank who?
Frankly my dear, I don't give a damn!

Knock Knock
Who's there?
Felix!
Felix who?
Felix my ice-
cream, I'll
lick his!

Knock Knock

Who's there?

Fozzie!

Fozzie who?

Fozzie hundredth time,
my name is Nick!

Knock Knock

Who's there?

Gotter!

Gotter who?

Gotter go to the toilet!

Knock Knock
Who's there?
Gladys!
Gladys who?
Gladys Saturday aren't you?

Knock Knock
Who's there?
German border patrol
German border patrol who?
Ve vill ask ze questions!

Knock Knock

Who's there?

Gary!

Gary who?

Gary on smiling!

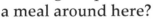

Just a
happy guy

Knock Knock

Who's there?

Genoa!

Genoa who?

Genoa good place to have
a meal around here?

Knock Knock

Who's there?

Goose!

Goose who?

Goosey Goosey Gander!

Knock Knock

Who's there?

Gopher!

Gopher who?

Gopher help, I've been tied up!

Knock Knock

Who's there?

Gorilla!

Gorilla who?

Gorilla cheese
sandwich for me,
please!

Knock Knock

Who's there?

Guinea!

Guinea who?

Guinea some money so I can buy
some food!

Knock Knock
Who's there?
Gus!
Gus who?
No, you guess who. I already know!

Knock Knock
Who's there?
Guthrie!
Guthrie who?
Guthrie musketeers!

Knock Knock
Who's there?
Grant!
Grant who?
Grant you three wishes!

Knock Knock
Who's there?
Gizza!
Gizza who?
Gizza kiss!

kissy
kissy
kissy

Knock Knock

Who's there?

Howard!

Howard who?

Howard I know?

Knock Knock

Who's there?

Harmony!

Harmony who?

Harmony electricians does it take
to change a light bulb?

Knock Knock
Who's there?
Haden!
Haden who?
Haden seek!

Knock Knock
Who's there?
Hair!
Hair who?
I'm hair to stay!

Knock Knock
Who's there?
Hammond!
Hammond who?
Hammond eggs for breakfast please!

Knock Knock
Who's there?
Hans!
Hans who?
Hans are on the end of your arms!

Knock Knock
Who's there?
Harlow!
Harlow who?
Harlow Dolly!

Knock Knock
Who's there?
Hacienda!
Hacienda who?
Hacienda the
story! It's
bedtime now!

Knock Knock

Who's there?

Havalock!

Havalock who?

Havalock put on your door!

Knock Knock

Who's there?

Heidi!

Heidi who?

Heidi ho!

Knock Knock

Who's there?

Hester!

Hester who?

Hester la vista!

Knock Knock

Who's there?

Hey!

Hey who?

Hey ho, hey ho, it's off to work we go!

Knock Knock
Who's there?
Hijack!
Hijack who?
Hi Jack! Where's Jill?

Knock Knock
Who's there?
House!
House who?
House it going?

Knock Knock

Who's there?

Haywood, Hugh and Harry!

Haywood, Hugh and Harry who?

Haywood, Hugh, Harry up and open the door!

Knock Knock

Who's there?

Hugo!

Hugo who?

Hugo one way,
I'll go the other!

Knock Knock
Who's there?
Ice-cream soda!
Ice-cream soda who?
Ice-cream soda neighbours wake up!

Knock Knock

Who's there?

Ike!

Ike who?

(sings) Ike could have danced all night!

Knock Knock

Who's there?

Ima!

Ima who?

Ima going home if you don't let me in!

Knock Knock

Who's there?

Ines!

Ines who?

Ines second I'm going to turn around and go home!

Knock Knock

Who's there?

Iran!

Iran who?

Iran thirty laps around the track and I'm very tired now!

Knock Knock
Who's there?
Ira!
Ira who?
Ira-te if you don't let me in!

Knock Knock
Who's there?
Ivan!
Ivan who?
No, Ivanhoe!

Knock Knock

Who's there?

Ice-cream!

Ice-cream who?

Ice-cream,
you scream!

Knock Knock

Who's there?

Icon!

Icon who?

Icon tell you another knock knock
joke! Do you want me to?

Knock Knock
Who's there?
Ida!
Ida who?
Ida hard time getting here!

Knock Knock
Who's there?
Icy!
Icy who?
I see your
underwear!

Knock Knock
Who's there?
Irish stew!
Irish stew who?
Irish stew in the name of the law!

Knock Knock

Who's there?

Ida!

Ida who?

(sings) Ida know why I love you like I do!

Knock Knock

Who's there?

Irish!

Irish who?

Irish I had a million dollars!

Knock Knock

Who's there?

Ivor!

Ivor who?

Ivor you let me in or I'll break the door down!

Knock Knock!

Who's there?

Irish!

Irish who?

Irish I knew some more knock knock jokes.

Ahhr... to be shur... to be shur... Ay cairnt think of one more knock-knock joke

Knock Knock

Who's there?

Jamaica!

Jamaica who?

Jamaica mistake!

Knock Knock

Who's there?

Jam!

Jam who?

Jam mind, I'm trying to get out!

Knock Knock

Who's there?

Jasmine!

Jasmine who?

Jasmine play the saxophone,
piano and trumpet!

Knock Knock

Who's there?

Jean!

Jean who?

Jean-ius! Ask me a question!

Knock Knock
Who's there?
Justin!
Justin who?
Justin time
for lunch!

Knock Knock
Who's there?
Jerry!
Jerry who?
Jerry can, even if you can't!

Knock Knock
Who's there?
Jess!
Jess who?
Jess me and my shadow!

Knock Knock
Who's there?
Jester!
Jester who?
Jester minute! I'm looking for my key!

Knock Knock

Who's there?

Jethro!

Jethro who?

Jethro a rope out the window!

Knock Knock

Who's there?

Jewell!

Jewell who?

Jewell know me when you see me!

Knock Knock

Who's there?

Juan!

Juan who?

(sings) Juan two three o'clock,
four o'clock rock!

Knock Knock

Who's there?

Jaws!

Jaws who?

Jaws truly!

Who's there ? ? ?
I hope it's not who
I think it is...

Knock Knock

Who's there?

Juno!

Juno who?

I know who, do you know who?

Knock Knock

Who's there?

Justice!

Justice who?

Justice I thought! You won't let me in!

Knock Knock
Who's there?

Java!

Java who?

Java dollar you can lend me?

Knock Knock
Who's there?

Jeff!

Jeff who?

Jeff in one ear, can you please speak a bit louder!

Knock Knock

Who's there?

Jim!

Jim who?

Jim mind if we come in?

Hi...
It's JIM here...
and 42 of
my best friends.
Can we come in?

Knock Knock

Who's there?

Kenya!

Kenya who?

Kenya keep the noise down, some of us are trying to sleep!

Knock Knock
Who's there?
Knee!
Knee who?
Knee-d you ask?

Knock Knock
Who's there?
Knock Knock
Who's there?
Knock Knock
Who's there?
I'm sorry, but Mum told me never to speak to strangers!

Knock Knock
Who's there?
Kent!
Kent who?
Kent you let me in?

Knock Knock
Who's there?
Ken!
Ken who?
Ken I come in?
It's raining!

Knock Knock

Who's there?

Kipper!

Kipper who?

Kipper your hands off me!

Knock Knock

Who's there?

Lettuce!

Lettuce who?

Lettuce in, it's cold outside!

Knock Knock
Who's there?
Lee King!
Lee King who?
Lee King bucket!

Knock Knock
Who's there?
Luke!
Luke who?
Luke through
the peephole
and you'll see!

Knock Knock

Who's there?

Len!

Len who?

Len me some money!

Knock Knock

Who's there?

Leonie!

Leonie who?

Leonie one for me!

Knock Knock

Who's there?

Les!

Les who?

Les go out for dinner!

Knock Knock

Who's there?

Lillian!

Lillian who?

Lillian the garden!

Knock Knock

Who's there?

Lionel!

Lionel who?

Lionel bite you if you don't watch out!

Knock Knock

Who's there?

Lion!

Lion who?

Lion down is the best thing to do when you're sick!

Knock Knock

Who's there?

Leif!

Leif who?

Leif me alone!

Knock Knock

Who's there?

Lois!

Lois who?

Lois the opposite of high!

Knock Knock
Who's there?
Lucinda!
Lucinda who?
(sings) Lucinda sky with diamonds!

Knock Knock
Who's there?
Lucy!
Lucy who?
Lucy lastic is embarrassing!

Knock Knock

Who's there?

Lass!

Lass who?

Are you a cowboy?

Knock Knock

Who's there?

Lisa!

Lisa who?

Lisa new car, furniture or computer equipment!

Knock Knock
Who's there?
Lena!
Lena who?
Lena little closer and I'll tell you!

Knock Knock
Who's there?
Larva!
Larva who?
I larva you!

YODEL-A-EE-OOO

Knock Knock
Who's there?
Little old lady!
Little old lady who?
I didn't know you could yodel!

131

Knock Knock

Who's there?

Letter!

Letter who?

Letter in or she'll knock the door down!

Knock Knock
Who's there?
Minnie!
Minnie who?
Minnie people would like to know!

Knock Knock
Who's there?
Midas!
Midas who?
Midas well let me in!

Knock Knock

Who's there?

Maia!

Maia who?

Maiaunt and uncle are coming to stay!

Knock Knock

Who's there?

Malcolm!

Malcolm who?

Malcolm you won't open the door?

Knock Knock
Who's there?
Mister!
Mister who?
Mister last train home!

Knock Knock
Who's there?
Manny!
Manny who?
Manny are called, few are chosen!

Knock-Knock
Who's there?
My panther.
My panther who?
My panther falling down!

Umm.... that LOOSE PANTS DIET certainly works

Knock Knock

Who's there?

Marie!

Marie who?

Marie the one you love!

Knock Knock

Who's there?

Martha!

Martha who?

Martha up to the top of the hill and marched them down again!

Knock Knock

Who's there?

Mary!

Mary who?

Mary Christmas and a happy new year!

Knock Knock

Who's there?

Matt!

Matt who?

Matter of fact!

Knock Knock
Who's there?
Matthew!
Matthew who?
Matthew lace
has come
undone!

Knock Knock
Who's there?
Miniature!
Miniature who?
Miniature let me
in I'll tell you!

Knock Knock

Who's there?

Mayonnaise!

Mayonnaise who?

Mayonnaise are hurting!
I think I need glasses!

Knock Knock

Who's there?

Meg!

Meg who?

Meg up your own mind!

Knock Knock

Who's there?

Mickey!

Mickey who?

Mickey is stuck in the lock!

Knock Knock

Who's there?

Mike and Angelo!

Mike and Angelo who?

Mike and Angelo was a great sculptor!

Knock Knock

Who's there?

Moppet!

Moppet who?

Moppet up before someone slips!

Knock Knock

Who's there?

Mortimer!

Mortimer who?

Mortimer than meets the eyes!

Knock Knock

Who's there?

Madam!

Madam who?

Madam foot got stuck in the door!

Knock Knock
Who's there?
Mandy!
Mandy who?
Mandy lifeboats, we're sinking!

Knock Knock
Who's there?
Mabel!
Mabel who?
Mabel doesn't work either!

Knock Knock

Who's there?

Noah!

Noah who?

Noah good place for a meal?

Knock Knock

Who's there?

Norma Lee!

Norma Lee who?

Norma Lee I'd be at school but I've got the day off!

Knock Knock

Who's there?

Noah!

Noah who?

Noah counting for taste!

Knock Knock

Who's there?

Noah!

Noah who?

Noah yes? What's your decision?

Knock Knock

Who's there?

Noise!

Noise who?

Noise to see you!

Knock Knock

Who's there?

Norway!

Norway who?

Norway am I leaving until
I've spoken to you!

Knock Knock

Who's there?

Nanna!

Nanna who?

Nanna your
business!

There are hundreds of perfectly good banks to rob... you great brute... ...so buzz off!

Knock Knock

Who's there?

Nose!

Nose who?

Nosey parker! Mind your
own business!

Knock Knock

Who's there?

Neil!

Neil who?

Neil down and take a look!

Knock Knock

Who's there?

Nicholas!

Nicholas who?

Nicholas girls shouldn't climb trees!

Knock Knock
Who's there?
Nobody!
Nobody who?
No body, just
a skeleton!

Knock Knock
Who's there?
Orson!
Orson who?
Orson cart!

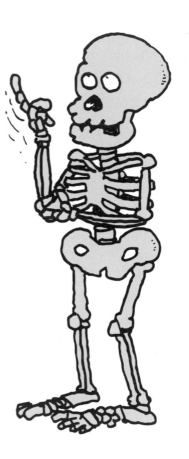

Knock Knock

Who's there?

Oboe!

Oboe who?

Oboe, I've got the wrong house!

Knock Knock

Who's there?

Olive!

Olive who?

Olive you!

Knock Knock
Who's there?
Offer!
Offer who?
Offer gotten who I am!

Knock Knock
Who's there?
Olive!
Olive who?
Olive in that house across the road!

Knock Knock

Who's there?

Oscar!

Oscar who?

Oscar silly question, get a silly answer!

Knock Knock

Who's there?

Ooze!

Ooze who?

Ooze in charge around here?

Knock Knock

Who's there?

Ocelot!

Ocelot who?

Ocelot of questions, don't you?

Knock Knock

Who's there?

Ogre!

Ogre who?

Ogre the hill and far away!

Knock Knock

Who's there?

Onya!

Onya who?

Onya marks, get set, go!

Knock Knock

Who's there?

Phyllis!

Phyllis who?

Phyllis a glass of water will you!

Knock Knock

Who's there?

Passion!

Passion who?

Just passion by and I thought
I'd say hello!

Knock Knock

Who's there?

Patrick!

Patrick who?

Patricked me into coming over!

Knock Knock

Who's there?

P!

P who?

P nuts, P nuts, get your fresh P nuts!

Knock Knock
Who's there?
Paine!
Paine who?
Paine in my stomach! I need some medicine!

Knock Knock
Who's there?
Police!
Police who?
Police let me in!

Knock Knock

Who's there?

Pa!

Pa who?

Pa-don me! Can I come in?

Knock Knock

Who's there?

Pa!

Pa who?

Pa-tridge in a pear tree!

159

Knock Knock

Who's there?

Parish!

Parish who?

Parish is the
capital of France!

Knock Knock

Who's there?

Parsley!

Parsley who?

Parsley mustard please!

Knock Knock
Who's there?
Pasture!
Pasture who?
Pasture bedtime, isn't it?

Knock Knock
Who's there?
Patty!
Patty who?
Patty cake, patty cake, baker's man!

Knock Knock

Who's there?

Paul!

Paul who?

Paul thing! Let me in and I'll comfort you!

Knock Knock

Who's there?

Packer!

Packer who?

Packer your troubles in your old kit bag!

Knock Knock

Who's there?

Pencil!

Pencil who?

Pencil fall down if you don't wear a belt!

Knock Knock

Who's there?

Paula!

Paula who?

Paula nother one! It's got bells on it!

Knock Knock

Who's there?

Pear!

Pear who?

Pear of freeloaders out here
wanting some dinner!

Knock Knock

Who's there?

Pecan!

Pecan who?

Pecan someone your own size!

Knock Knock

Who's there?

Percy!

Percy who?

Percy vere and you'll go a long way!

Knock Knock

Who's there?

Poker!

Poker who?

Poker and see if
she'll wake up!

Knock Knock

Who's there?

Phony!

Phony who?

Phony I'd known you wouldn't let me in, I'd never have come!

Knock Knock

Who's there?

Pier!

Pier who?

Pier through the peephole and you'll see!

Knock Knock

Who's there?

Pinza!

Pinza who?

Pinza needles!

Knock Knock

Who's there?

Polly!

Polly who?

Polly put the kettle on! I'm dying for a cup of tea!

Knock Knock

Who's there?

Phil!

Phil who?

Phil my glass up to the rim!

Knock Knock

Who's there?

Quacker!

Quacker who?

Quacker 'nother bad
joke and I'm leaving!

Knock Knock

Who's there?

Roach!

Roach who?

Roach you a letter but I didn't send it!

Knock Knock

Who's there?

Rabbit!

Rabbit who?

Rabbit up carefully, it's a present!

Knock Knock

Who's there?

Raoul!

Raoul who?

Raoul with the punches!

Knock Knock

Who's there?

Reed!

Reed who?

Reed-turn to sender!

Knock Knock

Who's there?

Renata!

Renata who?

Renata milk, can you spare a cup?

COME ON...! What about that mouldy turnip you're hiding behind your back?

Knock Knock

Who's there?

Robin!

Robin who?

Robin you, so hand over your cash!

Knock Knock
Who's there?
Red!
Red who?
Knock Knock
Who's there?
Red!
Red who?
Knock Knock
Who's there?
Red!
Red who?
Knock Knock
Who's there?
Red!
Red who?
Knock Knock
Who's there?
Orange!
Orange who?
Orange you glad I didn't say red?

Knock Knock
Who's there?
Rhoda!
Rhoda who?
(sings) Row, Row, Rhoda boat!

Knock Knock
Who's there?
Rose!
Rose who?
Rose early to come and see you!

Knock Knock

Who's there?

Roxanne!

Roxanne who?

Roxanne pebbles are all over
your garden!

Knock Knock

Who's there?

Radio!

Radio who?

Radio not, here
I come!

Knock Knock

Who's there?

Sawyer!

Sawyer who?

Sawyer lights on and thought I'd drop by!

Knock Knock

Who's there?

Scott!

Scott who?

Scott nothing to do with you!

Knock Knock

Who's there?

Shelby!

Shelby who?

Shelby comin' round the mountain
when she comes!

Knock Knock

Who's there?

Still!

Still who?

Still knocking!

Knock knock
Who's there?
Smore!
Smore who?
Can I have smore
marshmallows?

Knock Knock
Who's there?
Shamp!
Shamp who?
Why, do I have lice?

Knock Knock!

Who's there?

Stopwatch!

Stopwatch who?

Stopwatch you're doing and open
this door!

Knock Knock

Who's there?

Sancho!

Sancho who?

Sancho a letter but you never answered!

Knock Knock

Who's there?

Sally!

Sally who?

Sally duffer! It's just me!

Knock Knock

Who's there?

Stitch!

Stitch who?

Stitch in time saves nine!

Knock, knock.

Who's there?

Sombrero.

Sombrero who?

Sombrero-ver
the rainbow . . .

Knock Knock

Who's there?

Sabina!

Sabina who?

Sabina long time since I've been
at your place!

Knock Knock

Who's there?

Sacha!

Sacha who?

Sacha fuss you're making!

Knock Knock

Who's there?

Sal!

Sal who?

Sal long way for me to go home!

Knock knock.
Who's there?
Snow.
Snow who?
Snow good
asking me.

Knock Knock
Who's there?
Sally!
Sally who?
Sally days yet!

Knock Knock

Who's there?

Sam!

Sam who?

Sam I am, green eggs and ham!

Knock Knock

Who's there?

Samantha!

Samantha who?

Samantha others have already gone!

Knock Knock

Who's there?

Sarah!

Sarah who?

Sarah nother way in?

Knock Knock

Who's there?

Sari!

Sari who?

Sari I took so long!

Knock Knock.

Who's there?

Satin.

Satin who?

Who satin
my chair?

Knock Knock

Who's there?

Says!

Says who?

Says me!

Knock Knock
Who's there?
Scold!
Scold who?
Scold out here, let me in!

Knock Knock
Who's there?
Sadie!
Sadie who?
Sadie magic
words and
I'll tell you!

Knock Knock

Who's there?

Sherwood!

Sherwood who?

Sherwood love to come inside!
How about it?

Knock Knock

Who's there?

Shirley!

Shirley who?

Shirley you know by now!

Knock Knock

Who's there?

Sister!

Sister who?

Sister right place or am I lost again?

Knock Knock

Who's there?

Turnip!

Turnip who?

Turnip for school
tomorrow or there
will be trouble!

Knock Knock

Who's there?

Tish!

Tish who?

Bless you!

Knock Knock

Who's there?

Tank!

Tank who?

You're welcome!

Knock Knock

Who's there?

Turnip!

Turnip who?

Turnip the heater, it's cold in here!

Knock Knock

Who's there?

Tick!

Tick who?

Tick 'em up, I'm a tongue-tied towboy!

Knock-Knock

Who's there?

Troy!

Troy who?

Troy as I may, I can't reach the bell.

Knock Knock

Who's there?

Theresa!

Theresa who?

Theresa green!

Knock Knock
Who's there?
Tex!
Tex who?
Tex two to tango!

Knock Knock
Who's there?
Thistle!
Thistle who?
Thistle be the last time I knock!

Knock Knock
Who's there?
Tibet!
Tibet who?
Early Tibet, early to rise!

Knock Knock
Who's there?
Tamara!
Tamara who?
Tamara is Wednesday, today is Tuesday!

Knock knock.
Who's there?
Tuba.
Tuba who?
Tuba toothpaste.

Knock Knock
Who's there?
Tish!
Tish who?
Gesundheit!

Knock Knock
Who's there?
Tennis!
Tennis who?
Tennis five plus five!

Knock Knock
Who's there?
Toby!
Toby who?
Toby or not to be.
That is the question!

Knock Knock

Who's there?

Teddy!

Teddy who?

Teddy the neighbourhood,
tomorrow the world!

Knock, Knock.

Who's there?

U-2!

U-2 who?

U-2 can buy a brand
new car for only $199
a month!

Knock Knock
Who's there?
U!
U who?
U for me and me for you!

Knock Knock
Who's there?
Una!
Una who?
No I don't, tell me!

Knock Knock

Who's there?

Utah!

Utah who?

Utah the road and I'll mend the fence!

Knock Knock

Who's there?

U-8!

U-8 who?

U-8 my lunch!

Knock Knock
Who's there?
Vitamin!
Vitamin who?
Vitamin for a party!

Knock Knock
Who's there?
Venice!
Venice who?
Venice your doorbell going to be fixed?

Knock Knock

Who's there?

Voodoo!

Voodoo who?

Voodoo you think you are?

Knock Knock

Who's there?

Vaughan!

Vaughan who?

Vaughan day you'll let me in!

Knock Knock
Who's there?
Vault!
Vault who?
(sings) Vault-sing Matilda!

Knock Knock
Who's there?
Witches.
Witches who?
Witches the
way home?

201

Knock Knock
Who's there?
Willube!
Willube who?
Will you be my valentine?

Knock Knock
Who's there?
Water!
Water who?
Water friends for!

Knock Knock
Who's there?
William!
William who?
William mind your own business?

I'll come back again tomorrow... and the day after too.

Knock Knock!
Who's there?
Wayne!
Wayne who?
Wayne, Wayne,
go away, come
again another day!

203

Knock Knock

Who's there?

Woodward!

Woodward who?

Woodward have come but he was busy!

Knock Knock

Who's there?

Welcome!

Welcome who?

Welcome outside and join me!

Knock Knock

Who's there?

Wicked!

Wicked who?

Wicked be a great couple
if you gave me a chance!

Knock knock

Who's there?

Waiter!

Waiter who?

Waiter minute while
I tie my shoe.

Knock Knock
Who's there?
Wednesday!
Wednesday who?
(sings) Wednesday saints
go marching in!

Knock Knock
Who's there?
Who!
Who who?
What are you – an owl?

Knock Knock

Who's there?

Wooden shoe!

Wooden shoe who?

Wooden shoe like to know!

Who's the new Dutch boy down the end between the Italian girl and the Aussie rubber thong?

Knock Knock

Who's there?

Weirdo!

Weirdo who?

Weirdo you think you're going?

Knock Knock
Who's there?
Wanda!
Wanda who?
Wanda buy some cookies?

Knock Knock
Who's there?
Watson!
Watson who?
Watson TV tonight?

208

Knock Knock

Who's there?

Weed!

Weed who?

Weed better mow the lawn before it gets too long.

Knock Knock

Who's there?

Waddle!

Waddle who?

Waddle you give me to leave
you alone?

Knock Knock

Who's there?

Wenceslas!

Wenceslas who?

Wenceslas bus home?

Knock Knock

Who's there?

Woody!

Woody who?

Woody now be a good time to visit?

Knock Knock

Who's there?

Winner

Winner who?

Winner you gonna get this door fixed?

This is my door over here...

Knock Knock
Who's there?
Who!
Who who?
I can hear an echo!

Knock Knock
Who's there?
Wafer!
Wafer who?
Wafer a long time but I'm back now!

Knock Knock.

Who's there?

Wilma.

Wilma who?

Wilma dinner be ready soon?

Change the channel on the TV will you luv... my battery's dead again

Knock Knock

Who's there?

Xavier!

Xavier who?

Xavier money for a rainy day!

Knock, Knock.
Who's there?
X!
X who?
X-tremely pleased to meet you!

214

Knock Knock
Who's there?
Xena!
Xena who?
Xena minute!

Knock Knock
Who's there?
Xenia!
Xenia who?
Xenia stealing
my candy!

Knock Knock
Who's there?
Yah!
Yah who?
Ride 'em cowboy!

Knock Knock
Who's there?
You!
You who?
Did you call?

Knock Knock
Who's there?
Yul!
Yul who?
Yul never guess!

Knock Knock
Who's there?
Zombies.
Zombies who?
Zombies make honey, zombies just buzz around.

Knock Knock
Who's there?
Zeke!
Zeke who?
Zeke and you shall find!

Knock Knock
Who's there?
Zippy!
Zippy who?
Zippy dee doo dah, zippy dee ay!

Knock Knock
Who's there?
Zeb!
Zeb who?
Zeb been any mail delivered for me?

Knock, Knock.
Who's there?
Zany!
Zany who?
Zany body home?

Knock Knock
Who's there?
Zesty!
Zesty who?
Zesty home of Meester Jones?

Knock Knock
Who's there?
Zachary!
Zachary who?
Zachary one more minute
before I get mad!